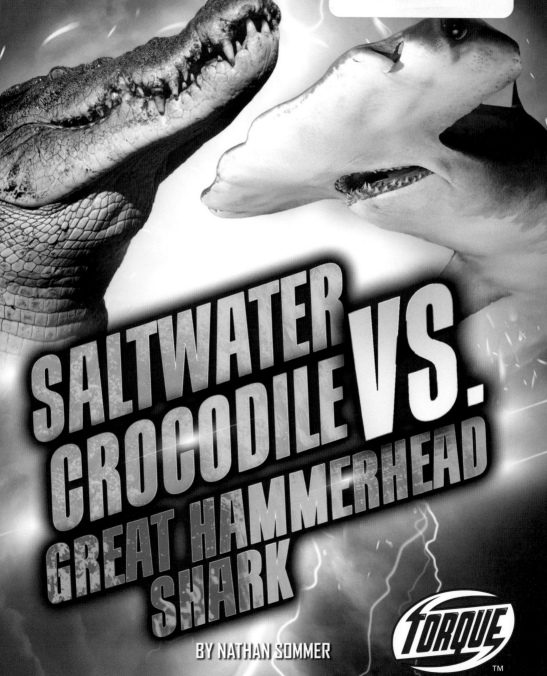

SALTWATER CROCODILE VS. GREAT HAMMERHEAD SHARK

BY NATHAN SOMMER

BELLWETHER MEDIA • MINNEAPOLIS, MN

TM

Torque brims with excitement
perfect for thrill-seekers of all kinds.
Discover daring survival skills, explore
uncharted worlds, and marvel at mighty
engines and extreme sports. In *Torque* books,
anything can happen. Are you ready?

This edition first published in 2024 by Bellwether Media, Inc.

No part of this publication may be reproduced in whole or in part without written
permission of the publisher. For information regarding permission, write to
Bellwether Media, Inc., Attention: Permissions Department,
6012 Blue Circle Drive, Minnetonka, MN 55343.

Library of Congress Cataloging-in-Publication Data

LC record for Saltwater Crocodile vs. Great Hammerhead Shark available at:
https://lccn.loc.gov/2023042538

Editor: Suzane Nguyen   Designer: Josh Brink

Printed in the United States of America, North Mankato, MN.

TABLE OF CONTENTS

THE COMPETITORS 4

SECRET WEAPONS 10

ATTACK MOVES 16

READY, FIGHT! 20

GLOSSARY............................. 22

TO LEARN MORE 23

INDEX 24

THE COMPETITORS

The world's warm, shallow waters are home to many beastly hunters. Among them, saltwater crocodiles are **apex predators**. Even large animals cannot escape the jaws of these giant **reptiles**.

Great hammerhead sharks are strong hunters, too. These huge sharks even eat other hammerheads! Which **predator** really rules the salty waters?

SALTWATER CROCODILE PROFILE

0 | 5 FEET | 10 FEET | 15 FEET | 20 FEET | 25 FEET

LENGTH
UP TO 23 FEET
(7 METERS)

WEIGHT
UP TO 2,200 POUNDS
(998 KILOGRAMS)

HABITAT

RIVERS

WARM OCEANS

SWAMPS

SALTWATER CROCODILE RANGE

RANGE

Saltwater crocodiles are the world's largest reptiles! They grow up to 23 feet (7 meters) long. The crocodiles can weigh more than 2,200 pounds (998 kilograms).

These beasts live in parts of Asia and Australia. They are found in both freshwater and saltwater areas. The crocodiles prefer rivers and swamps near coastlines.

A LONG HISTORY

Saltwater crocodiles have existed for over 200 million years!

Great hammerhead sharks are the largest hammerhead sharks. They grow up to 20 feet (6.1 meters) long. The sharks can weigh up to 991 pounds (450 kilograms).

These **solitary** sharks are named after their flat, wide heads. They have grayish-brown bodies with curved **dorsal fins**. These predators are found in shallow and open oceans worldwide.

GREAT HAMMERHEAD SHARK

```
0        5       10       15       20       25
        FEET     FEET     FEET     FEET     FEET
```

LENGTH
UP TO 20 FEET
(6.1 METERS)

WEIGHT
UP TO 991 POUNDS
(450 KILOGRAMS)

HABITAT

WARM OCEANS

GREAT HAMMERHEAD SHARK RANGE

☐ RANGE

SECRET WEAPONS

Saltwater crocodiles' strong tails make them great swimmers. They move their tails from side to side. This helps the crocodiles **lunge** quickly at **prey**.

STRONG TAIL

DISTANCE SWIMMERS

Saltwater crocodiles have been recorded traveling more than 559 miles (900 kilometers) by swimming.

Hammer-like heads help great hammerhead sharks find food. Sensors in their heads sense the movements of nearby prey. Their head shape also helps the sharks turn faster while hunting.

STRONG TAILS

POWERFUL JAWS

SHARP TEETH

Powerful jaws give saltwater crocodiles the world's strongest bite. Their jaws often defeat small animals with one snap. The reptiles lock larger prey in their jaws to hold them underwater.

Great hammerhead sharks use their wide heads as a weapon. They sometimes pin large prey to the seafloor with one side of their head. Prey cannot escape from getting eaten!

SALTWATER CROCODILE TOOTH

UP TO 5 INCHES (12.7 CENTIMETERS) LONG

Saltwater crocodiles have around 66 sharp teeth in their mouths. The teeth can grow up to 5 inches (12.7 centimeters) long. Their teeth sink deep into prey. Most victims cannot escape!

SECRET WEAPONS

SENSORS IN HEAD	WIDE HEADS	SERRATED TEETH

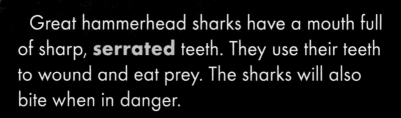

Great hammerhead sharks have a mouth full of sharp, **serrated** teeth. They use their teeth to wound and eat prey. The sharks will also bite when in danger.

ATTACK MOVES

Saltwater crocodiles are **opportunistic** hunters. They wait under the water's surface. Then, they **ambush** prey that come near the water!

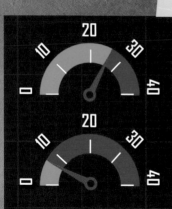

25 MILES (40.2 KILOMETERS) PER HOUR

GREAT HAMMERHEAD SHARK

6 MILES (9.6 KILOMETERS) PER HOUR

HUMAN

SPEEDY SWIMMERS

Great hammerhead sharks can reach speeds of up to 25 miles (40.2 kilometers) per hour!

Great hammerhead sharks use **stealth** to hunt. The sharks swim near the seafloor to search for food. They make a speedy attack once they sense a meal!

Saltwater crocodiles drag prey into the water. They hold their prey underwater until they drown. The reptiles roll to tear chunks of meat from large prey.

Great hammerhead sharks travel long distances in the summer. Some swim for hundreds of miles!

Great hammerhead sharks hunt many animals, such as stingrays and fish. They swallow small prey whole. The sharks hold down and bite larger prey into pieces.

READY, FIGHT!

A great hammerhead shark approaches a school of fish. It is about to feast. Suddenly, a saltwater crocodile snaps its jaws onto the shark's tail.

The crocodile tries to roll the shark. The shark turns and bites the crocodile with its serrated teeth. But the crocodile bites harder this time. The shark was no match for the crocodile today!

GLOSSARY

ambush—to carry out a surprise attack

apex predators—animals at the top of the food chain that are not preyed upon by other animals

dorsal fins—fins on sharks' backs that help them swim

lunge—to move forward quickly

opportunistic—ready to take advantage of a situation

predator—an animal that hunts other animals for food

prey—animals that are hunted by other animals for food

reptiles—cold-blooded animals that have backbones and lay eggs

serrated—having a blade like that of a saw

solitary—related to living alone

stealth—the state of being secretive or unnoticed

AT THE LIBRARY

Adamson, Thomas K. *Great White Shark vs. Killer Whale.* Minneapolis, Minn.: Bellwether Media, 2020.

Downs, Kieran. *Nile Crocodile vs. Hippopotamus.* Minneapolis, Minn.: Bellwether Media, 2022.

Drimmer, Stephanie Warren. *Sharks!: 100 Fun Facts About These Fin-tastic Fish.* Washington, D.C.: National Geographic Kids, 2022.

ON THE WEB

FACTSURFER

Factsurfer.com gives you a safe, fun way to find more information.

1. Go to www.factsurfer.com

2. Enter "saltwater crocodile vs. great hammerhead shark" into the search box and click 🔍.

3. Select your book cover to see a list of related content.

INDEX

ambush, 16
Asia, 7
attack, 17
Australia, 7
bite, 12, 15, 19, 21
color, 8
dorsal fins, 8
drag, 18
habitats, 6, 7, 9
heads, 8, 11, 13
hunters, 5, 11, 16, 17
jaws, 12, 20
lunge, 10
predators, 4, 5
prey, 4, 5, 10, 11, 12, 13, 14,
    15, 16, 17, 18, 19, 20
range, 6, 7, 8, 9
reptiles, 4, 7, 12, 18

roll, 18, 21
sensors, 11
size, 5, 6, 7, 8, 9, 14
speed, 17
stealth, 17
swimmers, 10
tails, 10, 20
teeth, 14, 15, 21
weapons, 12, 13, 15

The images in this book are reproduced through the courtesy of: Simon Says, cover (saltwater crocodile); frantisekhojdysz, cover (great hammerhead shark), pp. 2-3, 15 (serrated teeth), 20-21, 22-24 (hammerhead shark); Oceans Image/ Alamy, pp. 2-3, 20-21, 22-24 (saltwater crocodile); Danny Ye, p. 4; segalexplore, p. 5; Reezky Pradata, pp. 6-7; Izen Kai, pp. 8-9; Juergen Freund/ Alamy, p. 10; Michael Weberberger/ Alamy, p. 11; aeonWAVE, p. 12 (strong tail); taufankharis, p. 12 (powerful jaws); Vladimir Turkenich, p. 12 (sharp teeth); Richard Coulstock/ Alamy, p. 12; Greg Amptman, p. 13; Jean-Paul Ferrero/ Superstock, p. 14; Brent Barnes, p. 15 (sensors in head); Sail Far Dive Deep, p. 15 (wide head); Hakbak, p. 15; Media Drum World/ Alamy, pp. 16, 18; Martin Strmiska/ Alamy, p. 17; Andy Murch/ Biosphoto, p. 19.